LAZARUS INTERLUDE

A STORY OF GOD'S HEALING LOVE IN A MOMENT OF MINISTRY

REV. DENNIS O'NEILL
Introduction by Henri Nouwen

AVE MARIA PRESS   Notre Dame, Indiana

The poem "Lazarus" is excerpted from *Waymakers: Eyewitnesses to the Christ* by Sister M. Pamela Smith, SSCM, © 1982 by Ave Maria Press. Used with permission.

International Standard Book Number: 0-87793-271-9

Library of Congress Catalog Card Number: 83-60438

Printed and bound in the United States of America.

Cover and text design: Elizabeth French

With love and deep gratitude
to Kathleen and Bernard,
our parents on earth
and to Mary and Thomas,
our parents in heaven

Father Dennis O'Neill is an associate pastor at Christ the King parish in Chicago. Ordained in 1973, he earned his BA from Loyola of Chicago and his divinity and theological degrees from the University of St. Mary of the Lake in Mundelein, Illinois.

Acknowledgments

There are many more people than those mentioned in the text who are part of this story. In addition to the Christ Renews His Parish Women's Renewal Group I of Christ the King Church, whose prayers were such a source of sustenance, there are a number of others whose encouragement and support led me to record these happenings and to offer the final product for publication. Among them are Terry and Mary Childers, Bridget Courtney, Larry Craig, Agnes Cunningham, Irene Friend, Dennis Geaney, Lotte Gutmann, Jim Halstead, Richard Harris, Dick Issel, Dan Jenky, Rich LoBianco, Margaret Lorincz, David Miller, Dolores Murphy, Michael Murphy, Joe Pawlowski, Joe Piszczor, Frank Sasso, Bill Stenzel, Pat Tucker, Ursula Vaughan Williams, Joe Verardi, Luciano Verdoscia, Ann Wind, Rich Zborowski, and my pastors, Tom Fitzgerald and Ed Myers.

Special thanks to Peggy Kahn, whose editing skills helped me to translate a primarily poetic experience into prose; to my sister, Pat O'Neill, for all her secretarial assistance; and to Henri Nouwen, for his generous introduction.

Thanks too to Tom's family. For the sake of their privacy, I have changed his surname, the first names of his brothers and sisters, and the names of his pastor, his parish, and his hospitals. All other details are factual.

The gift you have
received,
give as a gift.

—*Matthew 10:8*

Introduction

Some time before Thanksgiving, Tom, a handsome 24-year-old, swallowed a bottle of sulfuric acid in a desperate attempt to end his problems. When he was brought to the hospital, his despair only deepened. Not only did he realize that death was imminent, but he also was convinced that God would punish him with eternal damnation. Two weeks later Tom died with the knowledge that God loved him deeply and would joyfully receive him in his heavenly home. Despair was turned into hope, rejection into acceptance, fear into joy, and resistance into surrender.

The days between Tom's angry suicidal act and his grateful surrender to God are described in this most unusual little book. It is the deeply moving story of two human beings whose care for each other allowed them to break through the boundaries of fear and to discover that love is stronger than death.

Whose story is this? Is it the story of Tom, who through the honest, spontaneous and generous care of Dennis, a young Chicago priest, became aware that he indeed was worth being loved? Or is it the story of a busy, hardworking priest, who was stopped in his tracks by a young dying man and came to realize that what really counts is giving and receiving love? Although Dennis wrote the story about Tom, it is as much the story about Dennis. Though it is the story about a new way of dying for Tom, it is also the story of a new way of living for Dennis. Though it is the story of ministry offered to a lonely youth, it is also the story of ministry received by a lonely priest. In truth, this is the story of the encounter of two men who at a critical moment in their lives are able to confess their need for each other and by so doing give each other new hope in the face of the inevitability of death.

But there is more. This is not only the story of Tom and Dennis. It is also God's story. I dare to say this, precisely because without it being God's story, there would be little more here than the sentimental event of two people who cling to each other in mutual need. It is Dennis' faith that gives a unique quality to his love for Tom. His attachment to Tom is real and very personal, but free from possessiveness. This freedom is rooted in his spiritual knowledge that as a priest he is called to let his love mediate a divine love which is greater, more powerful and lasting than his own. It is therefore very significant that Dennis could say to Tom: "In you, I had for the first time in my life met someone who was wide open to receiving all of my faith and all of my love." Without Dennis' faith this story would be little more than another "love story." Without his love this story might have been little more than another conversion story. But as a story of faith *and* love this story has become the story of God's healing love.

At first glance, Dennis' relationship with Tom appears very unprofessional. He seems to say too much too soon. He seems too eager to "save" Tom. He seems to get so involved from the beginning that it is unclear who is helping whom, and it seems that there is no or little concern to keep a healthy distance between the one who cares and the one who is cared for. Dennis plunges into Tom's life with an eagerness that may raise concern in the minds of those who read this story. But when Dennis tells us that he decides not to stay with Tom until he dies in order to be faithful to his promise to preach at a friend's first Mass, it suddenly becomes clear that from the very beginning there has been a larger, mostly undescribed context within which the risk of loving has been taken. It is the context of God's presence which becomes increasingly visible to both Tom and Dennis. This divine presence made it possible for them to become close so soon without fear of becoming overly attached and to leave each other without leaving each other alone. Dennis' story reveals in its unselfish spontaneity that the true minister, the real healer, the final life-giver is not another human being, but God himself. This truth, paradoxically, is not a reason for human distance but for human closeness, not for a refusal to become personally involved but for a carefree spontaneity in the expression of emotions and feelings, not for a restrained love, but for an uninhibited flow of affection. Precisely because Dennis knew about God's unconditional love, he could allow his own brokenness and need for love to become a part of God's healing ministry.

This little book says much about loneliness, fear, despair, and the deep human need for love. But it says even more about the mysterious possibility of letting these painful human experiences become gateways to the unlimited love of God. During the two weeks Tom and Dennis were together in mutual vulnerability, they both received new life. They both received it through each other, and they both recognized that not they, but the One who in his mysterious love had brought them together, was the true giver.

Henri J. M. Nouwen

It is a late November evening, and we buried you this morning. I am very tired right now, but I want to begin this at once, Tom, because we promised that we would never forget each other. I'll try to put down exactly what happened. As I told you then, it will surely be easier for you to watch over me than for me to remember you. From your place with the Lord you can be with me always, remaining close to me until that great day when I can join you with him. In the meanwhile I will have a few photos, the love of your family, and the memories recorded here—oh, such memories—to keep vivid my awareness of your constant loving presence.

For even the clearest, most intimate recollections fade with the years, blurring and becoming distorted. Even in the case of my mother, who died when I was 19, that's how things have gone. During the 15 years since her death, my memories of her have become so much a part of me, I can no longer see her clearly. Many of the memories of what we shared, she took with her.

I first heard about you on Sunday afternoon, November 15, when Florence Howard, a nurse in the intensive care unit at Cedar

11

Grove Hospital, phoned me. She and I have known each other for several years, though actually we haven't spent much time together: part of a weekend of recollection for nurses, her nephew Pat's ordination reception, and comparing notes on a few particularly desperate cases at the hospital. Now she had another one: She told me about you—a young man, age 24, who had swallowed a bottle of sulfuric acid and had somehow survived emergency surgery (though you would surely die, since you had no digestive system left, and most of your vital organs were no longer connected, having been sealed off from each other with scar tissue). She reported there was general consternation among the nurses, not only because of what you had done to yourself, but because your gentleness and sensitivity to what they were feeling had led them to care for you in a special way, and because you were presently sitting up in bed, calmly waiting to go to hell. She had phoned me, she explained, because she thought I had a gift for dealing with situations like yours, so wouldn't I please come out and talk with you.

I told her I would be glad to do so, but that it sounded like an emergency, and that there were several obligations I could neither cancel nor change and which would take most of the day. Would you live long enough? Or would she consider trying to get another priest in a parish closer to the hospital? She agreed to try, but this case required someone particularly qualified to deal with it. Although I questioned my qualifications, I promised to phone her as soon as my work was done, and if I was still needed, I would come at once.

You were on my mind all that day, and I began to find myself hoping that I would still be needed when I finally could come. I reached home at 11:15 p.m. and phoned Florence. No other priest had been available, so I prepared to leave immediately. In the meantime, she would let you know that I was on the way. It was then that she told me your name was Tom O'Toole.

On my way to the hospital I prayed. I tried to accept what Florence had said about my gift for dealing with such cases, and I told the Lord that I had no idea what was about to happen, but that I needed his help. So I asked him to take my life and to do with it whatever was required to benefit your life. Suddenly and quite unexpectedly I felt that he had accepted my offering, a feeling I have never had before with such conviction, and that somehow everything would be all right.

When I walked into your room and saw you, Tom, I could understand why the nurses were in such a state over you. Except for some burns on the tip of your nose and your lips and your tracheotomy, you were a picture of well-developed youth: the classic Celtic-Irish sort

13

with thick, wavy black hair, fine features, fair skin, blue eyes. Seeing this and imagining what was going on inside of you was hard to handle. Even though my mind didn't want to deal with it, my heart went out to you. Although you seemed calm, there was a look in your eyes that I shall never forget—frightened, haunted, expectant.

I introduced myself, and we shook hands. We exchanged a few statistics: You were 24; I was 34. We both grew up and were presently living on the southwest side of Chicago. . . . After a pause, I said that I heard you were worried about hell. You leaned over and wrote on a pad of paper, "My fault. I turned my back on my family and my country. I blamed others." I was amazed at your strength, Tom. The way you leaned over and wrote on the pad on the surface of the bed, I was sure you must have been in great pain, but you did it without even wincing.

When I asked you the name of your parish, you wrote, "Priest, Fr. Farley." Oh, St. Aidan Parish! We got back to the subject of hell, and you wrote, "I'm going there; I belong there." I replied that I had reason to doubt it, and to explain this, I reminded you of the story of the Father and the Prodigal Son. You were following every word, absorbing God the way a blotter absorbs ink. You wrote, "Can God be that good?" What a magnificent question, Tom!

14

Right to the heart of it. More because of your question at that moment than because of anything else, I knew that God *is* that good. More than ever before, I was convinced of it. You raised the right question, even as doubting Thomas once did, and the question, coming from you at that moment, resolved any doubt I ever had. I responded, "Tom, ever since I first heard about you this afternoon, I have been worried about you, hoping for you, praying for you, longing to be with you. If I could feel such concern for someone I hadn't even met, how much more must the Lord cherish you, the Lord who once said, 'If you, with all your sins, know how to give your children what is good, how much more will your heavenly Father give good things to anyone who asks him!' " (Mt 7:11).

You wrote, "My whole family: my uncle, my grandparents, and my godparents worked hard all their lives, and now their names are destroyed. My dad (was named) Thomas; so was his father. I wanted to be like him. He started to die in January (1972) and worked until June. He died July 2."

What a bind you were in, Tom! Ashamed to face either your dad in heaven or your mother on earth, you were ready to retreat to hell. I asked if hell could possibly be worse than what you had already been through. You nodded.

15

I reminded you of the parable of the laborers assigned to work in the vineyard at different hours of the day. I pointed out that even if you were called at the last hour, while your father and other members of your family had worked through the heat of the day, there was no problem about your all being rewarded in the same way by a God whose words in the parable made it clear: "I want to give this man who was hired last as much as I gave you. Don't I have a right to do as I wish with my own money? Or are you jealous because I am generous?" (Mt 20:14,15).

You wrote, "I was born 30th of October, Black Tuesday and Halloween. I honestly believe that I am evil." I reminded you of a blessed insight of our Hebrew ancestors in faith, recorded in the opening chapter of the Bible, although many people in every age have found reasons to doubt its truth. We read there that in the beginning, when God created the universe and all things in it, including *you*, Tom, he saw that it was very good.

I reiterated that you were not going to hell and, furthermore, I couldn't imagine any personal joy for me in going to a place from which you had been excluded. My heaven wouldn't be heaven without you. You began to cry, or you would have, if it hadn't been for your tracheotomy. You reached out with both arms

16

and we hugged each other. Then I knew that all would be well *and* that I was beginning to care about you so much that I was willing to do anything I could to make you happy here and to help you to be as ready as possible for heaven.

You had received the anointing of the sick and general absolution when you were first brought to the hospital, but now we went through these sacraments again, so you could consciously participate in them, and thus formally ratify the new closeness you were feeling in your relationship with the Lord. One thing I have come to appreciate much more deeply since ordination is the great power of all the sacraments—signs that, whenever given and received, are genuine opportunities for meeting with the incarnate Lord, who through sacramental ministry is ever willing to localize himself on our behalf, even as he did when he walked the earth.

You looked tired, and it was late, so I suggested that you get some rest, and I promised that I would be back the next day. I asked if you believed that I loved you. You nodded and wrote, "You're a good man. If only I had gone to church and confession, none of this would have happened. Thanks a lot."

On the drive home, I was grateful to the Lord for the way things had gone. He had accepted my offering of myself on your behalf. I began to know how Abel must have felt, the brother in Genesis (4:1-16) whose offerings found favor with the Lord. Then I realized that during my more than eight years in the priesthood, my perception of myself as an offerer of gifts to the Lord had been much more like that of the unacceptable brother, Cain. It's not that I haven't been happy in my ministry. Call it a Jansenistic sense that anything we enjoy in life must be evil simply because we enjoy it, or call it simply Irish puritanism or whatever you will, it's just that my awareness of my own sinfulness had left me feeling the *least* worthy member of the worshiping assembly. This didn't leave much room in my heart for the Lord's love to take possession.

A few weeks before I met you, Tom, I was approached by a woman who was enjoying becoming more actively involved in the parish but was ambivalent about doing so, as she felt that her lifestyle was too wrong. I told her I knew how she felt, that sometimes I sensed that some of the very things for which I was most grateful were also those for which I suspected I should be expressing regret to the Lord.

What had been a confused jumble to me was no longer so. I arrived back home, wishing that someone had done for Cain what you had done for me, Tom. Because you had accepted me, I knew that the Lord had also.

18

Monday
November 16

A busy day at the church, followed by a long evening meeting of our "Christ Renews His Parish" women's group. I had phoned the hospital earlier in the day and asked Florence to tell you that I would be coming after the meeting. She informed me that you had already thanked her several times for sending me. During the meeting, I told our women about you and asked them to join me in praying. We all prayed hard that evening, and we continued to storm heaven daily on your behalf. I'm sure those prayers helped, and you were pleased to know about them.

I was finally able to go and see you at about midnight. You still looked as strong as ever. You were writing on one of those magic pads you lift to erase. You smiled and wrote, "A miracle. After you left last night, I got two hours' sleep." I asked if you were in pain most of the time. You wrote, "When I woke up, no pain, but I began to twist around in the bed, and it began to hurt. But I want it to hurt." I went back over many of the things we had shared the night before. I told you that you did not deserve pain and that you really shouldn't make it hurt, because it would hinder any slim chance you might have of getting better. Thank God, you never got back on that subject again.

You took the pad and wrote, "It was so silly," referring to what you had done to yourself. Then you explained some of what had happened. On the previous Thursday afternoon, November 12, you went out to your garage, took up a bottle of sulfuric acid, which you had purchased for cleaning purposes, and swallowed its contents. Then, for no special reason, you decided to take a drive in the direction of Palos Hills, a good six to seven miles from your home! You managed to get that far when the police discovered you by your car, gushing blood. They rushed you to Cedar Grove Hospital, where emergency surgery was performed. The doctors said that it was incredible that you had survived at all, but in fact, apparently you were conscious and even able to sit up in a chair not long afterwards. Their prognosis was, and always remained, that you could not continue to live in your condition.

Tom, we will never know what prompted you to drive in that particular direction that day, but if you had not done so, we never would have met. Florence Howard was the only nurse who would have called me in on a case like yours. I know that you and I both believe that the Lord had a hand in it.

Since you had been writing a lot, I thought I would give you a rest while I told you more about myself, my family, and my parish work. Then you told me about your family: your mother, Kate, your older brother, Laurence, and the rest of your brothers and sisters: Kathleen, Bridget, Eugene, Maureen, and Anne. You remembered your early years as a happy time, secure in the love of your parents and close to your brothers and sisters. School presented no particular problems, and you and your friends enjoyed the typical experiences of growing up together until just before your sophomore year of high school when everything changed. That was the year your father died, and, for you, nothing after that would ever be the same again.

To an adolescent the loss of a parent can be overwhelming, particularly when it happens to be the parent of the same sex. For besides the shock of the forced and sudden termination of childhood, such youngsters are deprived of the example of the one best equipped to guide them through the troubled years of becoming adults. Another factor can play into the anxiety of a child with only one parent. It was brought home to me by the answers to a question submitted to my junior high class in personality development in my former parish where there was a high percentage of single-parent families. I had asked them what it was they feared most. A prevailing fear among those with but one parent, it turned out, was coming home one day and finding they had lost the other parent too. Nor did it help that your father's last instruction to you before his death was to take good care of your mother. It was probably something said on an impulse, because if he had meant it to be taken seriously he surely would have said something to your older brother, Larry, too. Alas, he could not have known how heavily this responsibility was to rest on your young shoulders, and how, at your age, you could not help but feel hopelessly inadequate to carry out such a directive.

When you finished high school, you didn't want to go to college, perhaps because you did not feel you could tolerate the separation from your family members yet. One evening when we were getting to know each other, I mentioned the difficult time I had adjusting to high school in the beginning. All the newness, both of the place and the people, was so frightening to me that I often paused on the back steps of my house before I could set out for the bus stop. From your response I realized that you had experienced similar fears.

College was not a good experience, and you came home after a year. The reasons are not altogether clear. Your ways of thinking and feeling were beginning to be at variance with those around you. You were extraordinarily generous and there were those who took advantage of your generosity, leaving you hurt and bewildered.

The next year—1977—was an extended period of depression for you. Some friends helped you to find employment; but because you felt it was wrong to be hired for any reason other than your own proven merit, you carried a sense of guilt about your good salary and complained to others that you were not working hard enough to earn it. After a short while, you quit the job. Even the responsibility you felt for supporting your mother and family was sacrificed to the integrity of the principles you lived by. Ironically, when you eventually found another job, it was of the same sort.

In July of 1980, you took a friend on a vacation out West. He had recently suffered a tragedy in his life, and you thought a break might cheer him up. The trip was such a great success that you and your family began to hope that *your* depressions might have passed too.

But by the end of the next month, it was apparent that more was troubling you than just conflicting principles. There was something radically wrong that was beyond your control. You would go through periods of incredible agitation when you couldn't sit still and no one could calm you down. Then you would move into phases of listless withdrawal when you were depressed, daydreamy, and noncommunicative. When you started wandering away from home inappropriately clad, your family felt they had no choice but to arrange for your commitment to a psychiatric ward for testing and diagnosis.

There seemed little doubt that your erratic behavior had a biological cause—a disorder in the catecholamines, the fluids that serve as neural transmitters in the brain, was the diagnosis. Massive doses of lithium were prescribed. One physician cautioned your mother that without the lithium there was danger that you might kill yourself or someone else.

Unfortunately, the lithium wasn't passing into your blood stream as it should have—not even when given in the highest possible doses. Even in liquid form, results were minimal. Your mood fluctuations became more frequent and more extreme. Finally, when you, who had always been the protector of the aged, pushed an old woman, it was agreed that you had to be forcibly restrained.

You were taken off lithium, and other drugs were tried. When things seemed to have equalized somewhat, you were released to your family with instructions that they continue to administer the drugs daily. During this time you tried so hard to function normally, returning to your job and resuming other aspects of the family routine, but still your behavior was unpredictable. One day you sent your entire paycheck to a missionary order. No one would have known except that you forgot to put a stamp on the envelope, and it was returned. Your mother especially hoped that your sense of humor, your wit, and your talent for making others feel good about themselves would pull you through. How much it meant to her when you resumed the familiar habit of walking into the kitchen, giving her a hug, a kiss, a twirl, and a big smile as you said, "Mom, who loves ya?"

Regular short visits to the hospital sustained you for a while, but the reprieve was short-lived. The old symptoms returned with a vengeance, so you had to be institutionalized in a psychiatric hospital, where you were treated for bipolar (manic) depression. Shortly after you were admitted, you tore a bathroom heater off the wall, so you were forcibly restrained again. The doctors began shock therapy, which they continued for most of the rest of your life. The apparent futility of all this treatment and the fact of its costing hundreds of thousands of dollars to the insurance companies tended to increase your depression. You tried hard to be a model patient, showing care for the other patients and the staff. And near the end of your stay in the hospital, you even befriended an old lady, whom you would take to lunch.

After nearly a year of institutionalization, you were released last July, so you could be one of your sister Kathleen's wedding attendants. Your grandmother recalls that during the nuptial liturgy, from her pew, she kept a constant eye on you, praying that you would make it through the ceremonies. She observed that you took many opportunities to steal glances at your mother. Apparently her presence gave you security, though I suspect you were worried about *her* security. You relaxed and had a grand time at the wedding reception. You even got your grandmother out on the dance floor for some of the faster numbers and gave her a workout, which she enjoyed thoroughly.

After the wedding, you stayed at home with your family. Any improvements were only minor and temporary. You were to return to the hospital for weekly shock treatments, but you didn't always go. You hated it that members of your family had to take time to drive you there, even though they were glad to do anything they could for you. In between treatments, you kept vacillating between being up and being down. You quit your job. Your friends tried to take you out to places to cheer you up, but they couldn't snap you out of your withdrawals. One thing that seemed to help was music, any kind of music from the loud contemporary sounds which you and your friends had formerly delighted in blasting during the parties you threw in the O'Toole basement to the lovely, sad Irish songs you could absorb and sing for

26

hours. I recall in the First Book of Samuel (16:14-23) about the depressions that would come upon King Saul and about how young David would soothe him by playing the harp. Alas, Tom, you had become so isolated that you would usually sing to yourself only when you thought no one was listening.

On Sunday, November 8, you told your family that you felt trapped by your situation. You said that you greatly desired to get your life back in order and that you were resolved to do just that. But the trapped feeling—the realization that neither you nor your family were ever quite sure what you might do next—must have been overwhelming to you: Because, apparently in despair of ever finding a cure for something you felt was an evil growing in you that you perceived as ruining your life and the lives of those you loved, you tried to burn the evil out of yourself by ingesting the acid. Once you had done this, however, you realized that you had only made matters worse. So now you began to consider *yourself* evil. That is the way you felt when we first met. You referred to what you had done to yourself as a "coward's way" and to yourself as a "mama's boy." These are things no one who knew you would have said about you.

On that late Monday night, you had a lot to share. I read what you wrote with great interest and asked only those questions whose answers might help to clarify what you were trying to say. When we were both too tired to continue, it was time to say good-night.

Tuesday
November 17

I made it a point to see you in the afternoon, because in the evening I was taking a friend of mine to an opera performance for her birthday. When I came into your room, I had a nice surprise. There was a smaller tracheotomy, so now you could talk! "Hi, Father," you greeted me, and I was delighted to hear something like your voice. We talked about your condition; still little pain, and all your vital signs were holding. Not even a fever! I told you that I had thought over your saying that you had taken the coward's way out, but that I was sure you were no coward. A coward would have chosen a much less painful way. Usually when you would say something negative about yourself, if I denied it immediately, you would be less receptive to my affirmations than if I simply listened at first, thought about what you had said for a while, and *then* denied it. In this case, you never called yourself a coward again. I commented on your physical strength and how it was serving you well in your present critical state. You indicated that it was the result of weightlifting.

You asked how my day had been. I told you more about my parish work, especially the youth center, and how I hoped that you might someday be able to help me with it. You smiled and said, "You're super." I replied, "So are you." But you shook your head. A while later, you looked at me and said, "I won't forget you." I asked whether you were planning on going somewhere. Again you shook your head. I assured you I would not forget you either.

As I left, I spoke to Florence. She reported that everyone was amazed at the way your vital signs were holding, but that by Thursday you would probably be in pretty bad shape. On my way to the opera, I was distressed by the thought of what you might have to face, and I pleaded with God for mercy for you. I promised that, if there were any way, with God's help, that I could love you into life, I would do it.

Wednesday
November 18

When I came into your room, you were sitting up smiling and wearing glasses. It was the only time I ever saw you wearing them. How opportune, because I had brought you something to read, an illustrated booklet about the life of St. Laurence O'Toole. I also brought a relic of the saint and gave it to you. I told you that your family's saint belonged more with you than with me.

We talked about different things, and then you leaned forward and began telling me that we would have to go to a hockey game one of these days. I asked if you played hockey. You nodded. I laughed and said that I could admire your ability in that regard, since all my life I had been pathetically uncoordinated in most sports. Suddenly you sat upright, swung your legs over the side of the bed, and stood up on the floor. You were nearly six feet tall! Since I had seen you only in a supine position until that moment, your height was a surprise to me. I grabbed hold of you and asked you to slow down; you were pushing recovery too fast. You did lie down again and then admitted that your stomach hurt somewhat. I asked whether you had stood up just to prove you could do it. You smiled and nodded. We were both hopeful and in good spirits that afternoon.

You mentioned a priest from Kerry who was a faith healer. I told you that I was afraid I didn't have that gift. I know that we were beginning to wonder whether there might be some hope that you could live. How I was longing for it, Tom! In you, I had for the first time in my life met someone who was wide open to receiving all of my faith and all of my love. I have been blessed with several good friends who are quite open to portions of both. Faith and love have always been two driving forces of my life, equal in importance, but you are the only one who could thrive on receiving both as one. In you both *were* one, and the more I gave, the more you were open to more. I found too I had more to give you than I could ever have imagined. We each knew that we were part of something miraculous. The question was just how many miracles would occur. I told you that I had to go home for supper and a youth center meeting but that I would see you later.

When I returned, you were not feeling very well: cold sweats, pallor, shakiness, but your vital signs were still holding. When I approached your bed, you reached out, took my hand, and said, "It feels good." This delighted me, because it meant you were becoming less uncomfortable with the attention being given you, even to the point of admitting that you enjoyed it. I had been holding your hand most of the time anyway, but from then on, I only let go when I was serving you in some other way. That evening, I spent much of the time mopping your forehead and changing cold towels. We still discussed the possibility of your surviving. I pointed out that if there were any chance of your recovering, it would probably be a long, hard road, involving more surgeries, a lot of pain, and who knew what else. Were you willing to do it, if you could? You nodded.

We even talked about how you might try to help others, especially young people, to reconsider before doing anything desperate to themselves. You liked the idea of assisting me with youth work, as you wanted to encourage young people to seek the strength they needed in life through faith. You yourself had always gone to church regularly and as an altar boy had been aware of a deep love of God when you used to serve Mass. Now you wanted to help others experience God's love as you were during this critical period of your life.

While I longed for your recovery, Tom, I was aware that recovery might lead to even more problems than those I had mentioned to you. You were beginning to depend on me, and this was a great step forward. Previously you had been so down on yourself that you couldn't accept being dependent on anyone: You hadn't believed that you were worth it.

Now that you could accept your own being lovable, if you lived long enough, you would probably need to revel in this dependence for a while before you could begin to realize the independence felt by people who are secure in love. Who knew how long the process would take for you? I was certainly willing to be with you through it all. But what if, as you began to feel better, you also began to suspect that you were too attached to me? Would you also think that I would be better off if you removed yourself from my life? What if, as you were getting better, something happened to *me*? Was what we shared a Romeo-and-Juliet sort of thing that could only remain beautiful under the threat of death? These things occurred to me. I also wondered whether we were like the old wineskins in the parable (Mk 2:22) that would burst when they were filled with new wine. No problem here. Somehow we were becoming new wineskins in the process. In fact, considering the way the good Lord seemed to be arranging everything each day, I was convinced that if you recovered, somehow all of this would be worked out.

Thursday
November 19

As usual I stopped at the nurses' station on my way to your room to inquire about your condition. The nurses reported that your blood platelets were going wild and you were running a fever.

Then your mother walked out of your room. I had never met her before, though of course I guessed who she was. I told her my name, and she gave me a big hug. Your sister Kathleen was with her. They were both elated over the changes in you and lavish in thanking me for my part in it. I pointed out that perhaps my main significance was in my being a stranger. After all, Tom, I wasn't saying very much to you that you hadn't heard already many times from your family. But since they are your family, you could always suspect that what encouragement they were offering came from a sense of familial obligation. Since I walked into your life a complete stranger, I obviously didn't have the investment in you that they did. I had nothing to gain by telling you anything but the truth.

They began to specify some of the more obvious changes in you. Previous to your taking the acid you had hardly any ability to concentrate or even to sit still. You couldn't read a newspaper, watch television, or converse beyond monosyllables. Now all that was altered. They brought me out to the waiting room to meet your brother, Larry, and your sister, Maureen. We all visited for a while.

That visit was a great relief to me. I had been quite worried about your family, hoping that someone was helping them work through everything. It was just as important for them to be able to cope as for you, Tom. But, since the time we two were spending together was making such a difference in you, I thought that I would use it best by giving it all to you. When I asked Florence about it, she responded that your mother had been heartbroken by the whole thing but that she also seemed to be handling everything well. Now, having met with her and talked with her, I knew that she was doing remarkably well, and I was relieved that she and the rest of your family thought that I could best help by going on with whatever was helping you. So I went to your room, confident that it was where I belonged.

You pointed to the St. Laurence booklet and said you had read two chapters. I told you that this would have to be a short visit, because I was running between parish appointments, but that I would return in the evening. You told me that I really didn't have to come again. I replied that I wanted to—I *needed* to. Although at this time we both still had some hope for your recovery, if things turned out otherwise, then we needed all the time together we could manage. We had already agreed that we would never forget each other. But, if you died, while it probably would be easy for you to be with me and to keep an eye on me, it would be difficult for me, because I wouldn't be able to see or hear you, not in the same way anyway. So we needed this time to absorb as much as we could of each other and to be as ready as possible for whatever lay ahead. You understood what I was saying and no longer fretted over my spending too much time with you.

When I returned that evening, after directing a wedding rehearsal and a choir practice, you were in pain and had the cold sweats. I spent the time wiping your forehead and your face and trying to help you cough up as much of the phlegm and necrotic tissue as you could without hurting yourself. For the first time, we talked about the afterlife.

I asked if you wanted to know what heaven would be like, and you nodded enthusiastically. So I shared with you all I could gather from Raymond Moody's *Life After Life* and what several people who have had "near death experiences" were able to remember about the period after their spirits had left their bodies. I added that it seems to be the common

37

testimony of most people who have had anything to say about heaven that it will be like a big celebration of love.

I suppose this celebration image has always meant a great deal to me, because I grew up in a home where we had many parties. Almost any events were reasons for celebration, including the wakes and funerals of any of our relatives from Ireland (which seemed to be nearly everyone who died during my first ten years). My parents and their friends used to have bimonthly Saturday night gatherings, rotating from basement to basement every fortnight of the year, except during Lent. Anyone could bring any guests they liked. Small wonder then that I grew up with the notion that the only *real* party was one where everybody was invited. My folks certainly seemed to know nothing about exclusion! So when I became a freshman in high school and they said I could have a party for my friends, I invited the entire class of nearly 300. I can imagine now what my parents went through the night of the party, but they never complained, and we repeated those parties twice annually until I went away to college. A few years after that, when I was in the theology graduate school, I remember having a difficult time imagining anyone excluded from heaven, and I still do. I was glad to discover that church fathers Origen and St. Gregory of Nyssa thought the same way; though, from what I know about their parents, they never threw the parties mine did.

Scripture is full of references to the effect that love alone will endure forever. One of the most precious gifts we have been given in this life is the time we can learn to invest in the lives of others. We have the Lord's guarantee that whatever of ourselves we give to others will live on in eternity in their hearts, in the heart of God, and in our own resurrection. This is so because we are creatures made in the image of God who is love (1 Jn 4:16), whose very life is an eternal exchange of self between Father, Son, and Holy Spirit, one in divinity because perfectly one in love. So with every effort to invest our lives in the lives of others, we not only grow in God's image but are already participating in his eternal life. Thus our personal resurrection actually begins in this life the first time we reach out to another human being and trust that we will neither be spurned nor rejected. For most of us, then, resurrection begins in childhood and continues throughout life as long as we struggle to resist our inclination to selfishness while managing somehow to reach out in love toward others, regardless of whether they can either accept or return it. The more we broaden the frontiers of our love, the more our lives will endure into eternity. In this way, by planting the seeds of resurrection, we also help the world to experience what is meant by the kingdom of God.

I shared these things with you, Tom, hoping that you would begin to realize how very much they applied to you, praying that you would come to accept what the rest of us already knew, that you were an extraordinarily loving and lovable person.

Suddenly it occurred to me that this blessed exchange of life for life, leading to a greater life, in which I believed and about which I had been preaching and teaching for years, was actually going on in a unique way between the two of us right then and there, while we were together, holding hands and looking into each other's eyes. I could feel the flow of this life, and those same hands and eyes seemed to be the main channels of the flow. Everyone could see the apparently dramatic way your life was being enhanced by our being together. If only they could have seen how gloriously, how miraculously, you were enhancing my life as well!

I did try to tell people, though most of them thought that I was just being kind. But you knew that something wonderful was happening, Tom. How grateful I was to our Lord at that moment for blessing us with each other and for blessing me with a realization of what was going on *while it was actually happening!* I wondered whether old Simeon could have felt more grateful the day that he recognized the child Jesus as the Messiah promised to his people (Lk 2:25-32).

While it is not essential that a loving person be a Christian in order to participate in personal resurrection, in every case, eternal life is a gift from God, possible only because Christ conquered death. So I also reminded you that evening of what Jesus was like when his disciples saw him after his resurrection from the dead; how he was not merely a spirit, because he continued to dine with his friends and was physically touchable. On the other hand, he was no longer restricted in any way by the laws of time or space, being able to appear and disappear at will and to walk through locked doors and walls. I explained that he was recognizable as their friend, Jesus, but recognizable in a way more penetrating than the one we usually use to identify those around us who are familiar and dear. In recognition we usually use our five senses, but with those we particularly love, there is also a recognition that comes from deep within the heart. When two people grow to love one another and spend a lot of time together, they begin to cherish little things about each other, perhaps a smile or the way the beloved says or does something; even a normally aggravating habit may become endearing because of the one who possesses it.

41

Whatever aspect of a loved one we will never forget, traits that will always make us smile in the remembering of them, stories that we will tell others about them again and again long after they have died, these are what will recapture for others, even though they may never have known the beloved one, not only what they were like but what they meant to us. Jesus and his friends loved each other deeply and shared these symptoms of love. For Mary Magdalene it was apparently the way Jesus said her name. Until he said "Mary!" her senses didn't help her much to identify him; at first she thought he was a gardener! For the two disciples on the road to Emmaus, as well as for many Christians down to this day, recognition of Jesus comes in the breaking of the bread. Tom, the evangelists recorded these things to say in as many ways as they could that love *is* the one thing that will endure into eternity. The first thing we will recognize in those we have loved in this life, when we meet them in the next, is whatever we most treasured about them when they were here. This applies to your own father and anyone else who has been particularly dear to you. We carry part of them in our hearts, as they do us. It is these parts, invested in love, that will always recognize one another and long for reunion. Heaven is that reunion.

After that it was very quiet in your room, Tom. You lay there, and I sat at your right side.

42

Then you looked at me and whispered, "I love you." "I love you, too," I responded. Then I remarked, "No one can say something like that on his way to hell." You smiled. It was getting late, so we said good-night.

Friday
November 20

It was a busy day at the church: a wedding and the reception afterward, then sticking around long enough to make sure that the youth center was securely chaperoned.

I arrived at the hospital in the evening. Your vital signs were a little better than they had been the day before, and you were not in much pain. But Florence reported that we were probably already going through the beginning of the end. You weren't using your tracheotomy to talk as much as previously. The necrotic tissues from your tongue, palate, and throat were continuing to slough off, so trying to talk was becoming more and more painful for you.

I spent most of the time that evening just trying to help you to feel more comfortable. You coughed continually so there was a lot of disposing of whatever came up, of holding your stomach while you coughed, washing your mouth out, wiping your teeth and your lips with my finger tips. (You really liked that!) All these little instances of care meant so much to both of us. It was significant too that you were also beginning to let your mother and the other members of your family do some of these things for you without your feeling self-conscious or constrained.

44

To pass the time, I talked to you about Ireland. Your father had come from County Leitrim, while your mother's parents were from Kerry. You had gone to these places with your father and Larry, and I had been there last August with my mother's sister, Sarah. Among the places associated with my family I mentioned Castlegregory. You repeated the word and smiled since you had been there too because your grandfather Fitzgerald came from the vicinity, while it was my great-grandmother O'Donnell who had once lived near there. This meant that you and I were practically relatives! I don't know why Irish-Americans feel the need to go through this routine, but it is quite common, and maybe we particularly enjoyed it because it was so normal. I held your hand until you drifted off to sleep.

Saturday
November 21

I had to spend the day preparing to preside over the evening liturgy for the feast of Christ the King. We were celebrating the 45th anniversary of the parish as well as the name day, so I had to prepare a special homily for the occasion. After Mass I made sure that things were running smoothly at the youth center and then headed for the hospital.

I can't recall much of what we shared that evening, Tom. It was a short visit anyway. Your vital signs were still holding pretty well, so I told you I wouldn't be staying very late. It was to be a busy day on the morrow: Besides big celebrations of the anniversary and the parish feast day, the bishop was coming in the afternoon for confirmation. Then there would be a reception for him afterward and a number of stops at different homes of parishioners. After that I would be out to see you again.

Sunday
November 22

When I finally made it to the hospital at around 9:30, your eyes lit up and you smiled. I told you all about how the day had gone. At the 9:45 Mass as part of the celebration, the head of the parish advisory board had given each of the priests and sisters a gift. We each received a small box containing a pewter figurine of a child leaning into the palm of a large upright hand and a holy card picturing the same figurine and inscribed with the words: "See! I will not forget you. I have carved you on the palm of my hand" (Is 49:15-16). I wanted you to have them. You shook your head no at first, but I persuaded you at least to keep the holy card. You smiled and took it.

One of the nurses came in and asked me if I could take a few moments to anoint an old lady who had been brought in earlier with a heart attack. After I visited with her, I stopped in the waiting room to see your mother, your aunt Maura, and your uncle Mike. They were discussing an article that had appeared in the news which claimed some scientists had succeeded in tracing the cause of bipolar depressive psychosis to a disorder of the chromosomes, which would seem to indicate that this illness was hereditary in origin. Your mother was convinced that it was through her that the disease was passed on to you. I pointed out that my family was prone to cancer and that my mother had died of it, but even were I to die of the disease, it did not follow that my mother should regret my having been born.

A few minutes later, I returned to your room. You smiled and said, "You should be proud that one person can make such a difference." I replied, "Not proud. Grateful. Equally grateful to you and to God," and I meant that with all my heart.

It was getting rather late. You knew how tired I was and kept encouraging me to go home. When I finally did, I pointed to the box containing the figurine and remarked, "I think I'll leave this with you." This time you did not refuse.

Monday
November 23

After 6:30 a.m. Mass I went back to bed for a while. The others in the rectory must have had some idea how tired I was, because no one woke me up. I slept until noon and was most grateful for this thoughtfulness. There was usually so much to do on any morning that someone must have taken over for me. I had parish duties that kept me busy in the afternoon and another parish renewal meeting in the evening. The women questioned me about you and told me to tell you that they were still praying hard for you. During the course of the meeting, one of the women shared with the group a quote from St. Catherine of Siena, which she said had often helped to sustain her during difficult times: "God writes straight with crooked lines." This seems to be precisely what God was doing with us, Tom. The group insisted that I leave the meeting early because they thought it was more important for me to be with you than with them. I arrived at the hospital at about 10:30.

When I entered your room, your mother was sitting with you. She smiled and told me that she was now allowed to be with you until midnight when the shift would be changing. I was delighted. Until then she and the other

49

members of your family had only been allowed five or ten minutes with you every two hours. Now, apparently the hospital staff thought both you and your mother could profit from spending more time together. For they were aware that you were no longer ashamed to face her and that she was overjoyed with the changes in you.

She got up to leave because she wanted you and me to spend the time together, and, though I urged her to stay, she wouldn't hear of it.

You looked about the same as you had the day before, but now you had some bloodstains on the gauze under your tracheotomy. I pointed to it and asked if it had started that evening. You nodded. And was it hurting more there? Yes. I reached out to take your right hand which was clenched in a fist. When you opened it, the little pewter figurine dropped out onto the bed. I looked up at you, and you broke into a smile.

While I was changing your cold towels a while later, I explained that I was going to visit a friend in the neighborhood and that your mother would visit with you for as long as she could. I would be back by the time she had to leave.

When I got back your mom had just left. Again you started coughing up blood and necrotic tissue, and this happened with growing frequency. The more you coughed, the more you hurt. Your blood pressure was starting to go crazy and your fever was rising. I was sure you were going to die that night, and I conveyed this to you by saying, "Tom, I think you will be meeting your dad before this night is over." You were ready. In fact, at this point, you were perfectly willing either to live or to die, calmly, even happily, welcoming either prospect. I suggested that your dad must be very proud of you; you were becoming the one thing that everyone is meant to be—a saint. I added that I knew you had been as proud of your dad as I had been of my mom and that, at her funeral, I'd counted the cars in the procession as a way of reminding myself of how many people's lives she had touched. I bet that you had done the same thing in your dad's case, and you admitted that you had. So I said, "You'll have even more, Tom."

Did you want me to have your family called? You didn't. I hadn't wanted to leave you anyway, but now I was resolved to be with you when you died. I certainly did not want you to die alone. So we stayed together for a long night of cleaning up blood and changing cold towels and linens. Of course, I was glad to be able to help you that way, Tom, but it was also heartbreaking to know you were in such constant pain.

During a period of relative calm that night,

as I was sitting there next to you with you holding my hand tighter than usual, I asked whether you would help me to get to heaven. You nodded. "It will be harder than you think," I said. I asked if you would help me with my work. Affirmative. "Good," I responded, "then I will try to make sure that the things you want done in this life will be finished. If you will be with me, we can work together." You smiled. "Sometimes . . . just sometimes . . . I am lonely. When those times come, will you be holding my hand, Tom?" You squeezed tighter.

A little later, after one of your coughing bouts, we prayed. You had already been anointed, so now you made a profession of faith. I asked if you would like a song. Your eyes lit up. Then I sang "Be Not Afraid."

> You shall cross the barren desert,
>   but you shall not die of thirst.
> You shall wander far in safety
>   though you do not know the way.
> You shall speak your words to foreign men
>   and they will understand.
> You shall see the face of God and live.

> Be not afraid. I go before you always.
> Come follow Me, and I will give you rest.

> If you pass through raging waters
>   in the sea, you shall not drown.

52

LAZARUS INTERLUDE

If you walk amid the burning flames,
   you shall not be harmed.
If you stand before the pow'r of hell
   and death is at your side,
Know that I am with you through it all.

Blessed are your poor,
   for the kingdom shall be theirs.
Blest are you that weep and mourn,
   for one day you shall laugh.
And if wicked men insult and hate you
   all because of Me,
Blessed, blessed are you! *

You listened carefully to every word and said, "That was beautiful." I told you that I loved you and that you were as ready as anyone could be for heaven. I was standing next to you at the head of your bed at that time, wiping your forehead. I looked into your eyes and said something that amazed me: "Tommy, it seems that the Lord wants me to stick around here for a while longer, but if I could, I would be glad to die and go with you right now. It would be wonderful being there with you. Do you believe me?" You nodded. "Good," I concluded, "because I have never said that before to anyone else, and I never meant anything more sincerely in my whole life."

Then I realized that at the same time I was preparing you for death, through your terrific receptivity, the Lord was also preparing *me* for death! I was as ready as you were! Despite the fact that there are many people I love here on earth, and many things I hope to do before I die, as dawn approached on that Tuesday morning, I would have been perfectly content to go with you to meet the Lord without any fear, without regret, without even a farewell. It's not that in the past I had ever been especially afraid of dying, but this was a feeling that went way beyond mere lack of fear. I could hardly wait! And you knew it, Tom.

I have never felt as fully alive as I did on that night when we both faced death together with a smile. I appreciated more deeply than ever before how true it is that death and resurrection are two sides of the same reality. And, recalling the saying of St. Irenaeus that the glory of God is man fully alive, I realized that together *we* were becoming a facet of God's glory.

It occurred to me later that Saints Augustine and Monica must have shared a similar experience when they spent an afternoon together in Ostia shortly before she died. Neither of them knew she would die two weeks later, but on a certain lovely day, while he and she were leaning out a window looking into the garden, they experienced an ecstatic sharing of what heaven would be like and how much they looked forward to it. It was such a significant memory to him that he later recorded it in his *Confessions* (IX:10).

As it neared 6:30 a.m., I heard your mom phone the nurses' station. I relayed to you that it looked as though you were going to make it through the night after all, and that you would be seeing your mother again. Good! You would be delighted to see her! I told you that she would be coming shortly and that I had to get back to Christ the King for the 7:30 Mass, but that I would return to you in the afternoon.

Tuesday
November 24

After morning Mass, I had to bring communion to several invalid parishioners. Then I came home, lay down on my bed, and had a good cry. I wept for your pain and for my own pain that I would shortly lose you to death—but also for another young man, the brother of one of our parishioners, who had taken his life a month before, for Jamie Butterfield, one of our teens, accidentally stabbed to death eight months before, and for the 23 other young parishioners who had died tragic deaths through the years and whose names are inscribed on a plaque in our youth center. How hard it is for young people to make it to adulthood! What suffering can be part of even the happiest lives! Lord, how I wept that morning! But even this turned out to be another gift given to me because of you, Tom. Tears. I hadn't shed any in the 15 years that had passed since the cry I had on the day my mother died. I knew that it would happen some day, and I had always suspected that something truly beautiful would bring it about. Of course, I never imagined that it would be anything like this. Who would have believed that God could have brought such beauty out of such horror!

    I got back to the hospital about 1:30 in the

afternoon. A nurse stopped me on my way into your room and explained that they had been giving you heavy doses of morphine since that morning, and that right now you were sitting up fully conscious and quite calm. You would probably remain that way until you would cough once too often and either your tracheotomy or the sutures in your stomach area would give way, and that would be the end. The end could come at any moment. Most of your family were with you, and they knew what was happening.

When I entered your room, all was quiet. Your mom was sitting on the edge of your bed, holding your right hand, and Kathleen was on the other side, holding your left. She got up and insisted that I take her place, while she stood by your mom. The vigil continued in silence.

Then I asked whether you wanted me to complete the prayers for the dying which we had begun the night before. You nodded. I read that beautiful prayer which includes the words, ". . . go forth, faithful Christian. May you live in peace this day with God. . . ." We all prayed together, united in the solemnity of that moment.

Your mother told me that you had requested that I preside at your funeral. I said I would be honored. She smiled at you and said, "Soon we'll be praying to you, Tommy." You didn't say anything, but you didn't look very comfortable with the idea either. You had only recently given up on the idea you were going to hell, and now already you were being treated like a saint!

You were resting calmly, coughing only occasionally, and now no more blood was coming up. As we were sitting on either side of you, I began to talk to your mother about my family. I told her that I have a brother, also named Tom, who, in some ways, reminds me of you. When my mother died, he was the same age as you were when your dad died. Just as in your case, it left him an exceptionally gentle person who has always been careful to avoid hurting anyone. I guess the death of a parent early in life may have this effect, as it seemed to affect my sister, Pat, the same way. Unfortunately, sometimes such gentle people are hard on themselves. In his book, *The Savage God,* A. Alvarez mentions several famous writers who lost their fathers when they were young and then eventually took their own lives. I talked about my family in front of you deliberately, Tommy, because I wanted you to overhear and to realize that you were not alone in what you had suffered through losing a parent. We talked very quietly, and you listened with great interest.

It was getting near supper time, and I had a youth coordinating board meeting that evening, so I headed home. Since I couldn't keep my eyes open during the meeting, they were kind enough to tell me to go to bed.

Wednesday
November 25

I phoned the hospital in the morning and was delighted to hear that you were still holding as stably as when I had last seen you. I had to teach that morning, so I asked the nurse to let you know that I would see you in the afternoon.

I remember that I drove to the hospital thrilled that we would be able to see each other again but wondering why you were still alive at all. You should have been dead on the first day. You should have died Monday night. You should have died yesterday, and yet you were still very much alive and still fully aware of what was going on. So many miracles already! There was no doubt that *you would die,* and as far as I could tell, you were as ready as anyone could be. So what more did the Lord have in store for you? Or for us? I suspected that there might yet be even more to this period of miracles. And I was beginning to consider myself a character playing a part in an autobiographical story being told by God. Even though the narration depended on my cooperation, it was God's story all the same. And I was so caught up in it that I was almost as eager to tell others about what had happened thus far as I was to find out what would happen next. I wondered too whether Jesus' disciples hadn't felt the same during the period when he was appearing to them between his resurrection and his ascension into heaven.

When I entered your room, you were alone, and you looked preoccupied. I asked whether you were frustrated at still being alive. No. Were you frightened? You nodded. Was the fear more about dying in general or the moment of death in particular? It was the moment of death you were worried about. So I described exactly how the doctors expected you would die, that you would feel little pain before it, and, of course, no pain after it. No pain ever again. I also reviewed with you all the thoughts we had already shared about death and afterlife, and this seemed to help you.

I mentioned that I knew you had been embarrassed yesterday when your mom said we would be praying to you soon. I explained, "You shouldn't be, Tom. She just meant that we will all continue to talk to you, and you *do* want *that,* don't you?" Yes, you did.

Then I knew that it was time to tell you something I had been putting off bringing up for days. On Friday morning I would have to fly to Lebanon, Missouri, where a good friend of mine was to be ordained a priest for the Diocese of Springfield. I was expected to preach the homily at his first Mass on Saturday evening, so there was no way I could avoid going. I would have to be away from Chicago from early Friday morning until some time Sunday afternoon. I hadn't wanted to tell you too soon, because I did not want you to rush dying in order to get your funeral over before I left. Now that it was too late for that, I wanted to tell you early enough so we could prepare for a two-day break.

I told you. Then I added, "You know that I really don't want to leave you at all, don't you, but that I have no choice?" You nodded and smiled. "Thank God," I thought, "everything will be all right." You took it very well, Tom. Then I had to go back to the church for a while, but I told you I would return just after I closed the youth center at 9 o'clock.

As soon as I was free, I drove back to the hospital. Your vital signs were still holding, and you were calm and still coughing no blood. I knew you were in pain, though, because your nurses kept asking you whether you wanted more morphine, and you never refused. They asked each time whether you wanted a large or a small injection. You usually took a small one. The dressing changes were growing more frequent, because blood was seeping out of the drains in your stomach. Not much was said. By now, most of our communication was nonverbal.

As midnight approached, I stood up to wipe your forehead. You coughed and, as usual, I held my right hand against your stomach to modify the pain a bit. You took it in your left hand, so I continued to lean over the bed. Your right hand was secured to a board in order to keep your intravenous tubes in place. You slowly raised that hand to my cheek and said, "You're such a man." I paused a moment, marveling at how much you had grown in your understanding of that word. Then I replied, "So are you, Tom." You shook your head no, but you kept smiling. "Good!" I thought, "with that smile on your face, at least you're not entirely rejecting the possibility." And I told you that you had a knack for saying unexpected things to me that kept making me accept myself in new ways.

A little later, while I was placing a cold towel on your forehead, I said, "You know, Tom, it's important to a lot of people to know that, in this life, they are the most precious persons in the life of at least one other human being." You nodded. I added, "Tommy, you mean more to me than anyone else." I asked whether you had been lonely the day you swallowed the acid. You nodded (I asked you the same question on the first evening we met, and you denied it). I assured you, "You'll never be lonely again." I asked whether your taking the acid had been a sin. You shook your head no. I responded, "That's right. Only a mistake."

I asked whether you loved your family. You nodded. "And your friends?" You nodded. "And me?" Affirmative. I inquired whether you knew how much we all loved you. You did. I asked whether you had any idea how your life was touching the nursing staff and other people in St. Aidan and Christ the King parishes, most of whom you had not even met. You nodded. I continued, "Tommy, do you have any idea how *special* you are?" You nodded. By this time you were smiling radiantly and gazing beyond me into another world.

I sat down for a while and rejoiced in that radiant smile, thanking God with all my heart that he had let you live long enough to realize your own goodness as well as his.

Since it was well beyond midnight, I stood up and wished you, "Happy Thanksgiving!" I gave you a kiss on the cheek and suggested that you better get some sleep, that, as usual, I would hold your hand until you dozed off. Then I would go home and get some sleep myself. I sat there holding your hand for about half an hour, but you couldn't get to sleep; you were too happy. I remarked, "This isn't going to work, is it?" You smiled and shook your head. So I said, "Good-night," and promised to spend the next evening with you.

Thursday
November 25

In the morning we had three church services. My brother and Karen, his wife, were having dinner for the family, so I spent the afternoon with them. I told them all about you, so they were very understanding when I excused myself to go to the hospital.

I arrived there at about 6:30. Your mother and your sister Bridget were in the waiting room. We exchanged holiday greetings. Then I headed for your room. On the way there, I overheard two nurses talking about you.

Of course, the nurses had been going through a lot of reflecting on and reacting to your situation. During your first days at the hospital, some of them had been hesitant in approaching you. They knew about your physical prognosis, but they had no idea of the psychological and emotional state you were in. When they did meet you, however, you had a way of setting them immediately at ease. You showed them such warmth and tenderness that they found themselves caring a lot about you and truly distressed at the thought that you were dying. One of them, Nancy, was particularly good to you, and, often without realizing it, she reinforced many of the positive things

65

I was saying to you about yourself. Not long ago, she was kind enough to send me a note in which she wrote, "It was wonderful having you on the team (or was I on yours?)" The awareness that you were growing happier and more peaceful every day was spreading among the staff and having such a positive effect on them that they began to accept your approaching death with unusual serenity.

But, unfortunately for them, not all of the nurses met you, Tom. And some who knew about you only indirectly were having a hard time dealing with what you did. One considered the whole thing a "cop-out" and was angered over the waste of a life as precious as yours. I overheard Florence trying to help her to view it differently. Then too some were struggling with the religious questions that emerge when suicide is discussed. One of the two nurses I overheard on my way to your room was expressing her delight that you no longer thought you would be going to hell. But the other retorted, "Well, isn't he?"

"Of course, he isn't," I thought, "and he probably wouldn't have gone to hell even if he had died the moment he drank the acid." Hell is a deliberate choosing to live in total, eternal isolation. And anyone who knew you, Tom, would say that there was nothing in your life that would indicate that this was true in your case. In fact, your ingesting the acid was an attempt to *break the isolation* you were feeling. This is often the case with people who take their own lives. They are surrounded by others who really care about them; but for some reason, often entirely beyond their control, they are unable to appropriate love. They can give it, but something blocks their ability to receive it. Inasmuch as there is a blockage of this sort in their affective lives, they are unwell and are less than fully responsible for their actions. And if they are not fully responsible, neither are they fully accountable.

You yourself never once said you had intended to kill yourself. You said that you had been growing more and more depressed because none of your treatments had succeeded in removing whatever in you was ruining your life and the lives of those you loved. So you decided to try burning it out—obviously not the clear thinking of a well man. You also said that once you started doing it, you couldn't stop yourself until it was too late. But in your case, of course, it was too late only in one way. Your extra two weeks of life here were certainly a rare blessing. And to be so prepared for heaven! What a gift!

But since, in his mercy, the Lord would surely have taken good care of you even if you had died at once, your miracle was an even greater gift to all of us. I don't take this gift for granted because I can compare our time spent together with the one other time in my ministry when I went through a daily preparation for death with another person.

It happened about seven years ago, while I was ministering in another hospital; and it was an old woman who had been given one month to live. I had known her from other times she had been in the hospital, and so I was aware that her life had been a rather unhappy, empty one and that her faith had only recently come to mean anything to her. It seemed to me that she had a lot of living to do in a short time, so I resolved to be with her part of every day for as long as she lived. She died a month and a half later a happy, peaceful woman. And that's all there was to it. But when I met you, Tom, a similar resolution brought miraculous results.

Of course, not everyone approaches death with a drastic need to live life quickly and deeply, though a saint like Mother Teresa of Calcutta can find and minister to such people every day. The significant person at this critical time in your life didn't have to be a priest, Tom, and it certainly didn't have to be me; but I will always be grateful that it was.

When I arrived in your room Thanksgiving evening, you weren't as peaceful as the night before, and the constant doses of morphine had reduced you to a pretty groggy state. Although you needed the morphine, I know you hated being sleepy during our visit. Also you were aware I would be going to Missouri in the morning, and I think that it distressed you. You were restless, though you were generous enough never to attribute it to my imminent departure. In most of our communication that evening, very little was said. You were bleeding more from the stomach, which meant that your dressings and the rest of the linens had to be changed even more frequently than before. I know that this rolling you over was painful for you. During the changes, I would hold you while the nurse did her work.

Your sister Bridget came in and sat with you. She hadn't had much of a chance to be with you, so I just did odd jobs around the room for a while. Finally, I sat down next to you. I no sooner hit the chair than your hand reached out and grabbed mine, holding on tight. You had that preoccupied look in your eyes that always let me know when something was bothering you, and when Bridget went out to be with your mom, I asked what you wanted. You weren't able to tell me, so I gave you your pad, which you hardly used anymore; and in a shaky hand you wrote, "Larry." Oh! You wanted your brother? Yes. So I went out and told your mother. She had quite a time tracking him down at work; but eventually she got through to him, and I could assure you that he was on his way. This seemed to help, but we never did find out just why you wanted him that night.

A little later, I told you that I admired you tremendously for the strong, courageous way you had been handling yourself throughout everything. You smiled. I added, "So *now* who's a man?" I was so taken with the sudden twinkle in your eyes that I almost missed it when you raised your other hand and pointed your thumb at me.

Despite the light moments, you still looked preoccupied with something. So I asked you again, "Tommy, what would you like me to talk about?" "God," you replied. And that was the last word you ever said to me.

Just then the nurse came in. It was time to change your linens again. She asked whether you wanted more morphine. Yes. A big injection or a small one? A big one, you indicated. So, even as she was giving you the shot and we were changing the linen, I reviewed the parables of the Father's love: the Father of the Prodigal Son, who did not care what his son had done but only wanted him back home; the generous master of the vineyard; the love of the Good Shepherd, who wants us all to be happy together. I talked fast because I knew you would fade quickly, and you did. You were already in a deep sleep by the time we finished changing the linen. It was 1:00 a.m., so there was nothing more to do than kiss you on the forehead, say, "Good-night, Tom," and leave.

I said good-night to your mother and your

brother, Eugene, and I told them I would be back Sunday afternoon. On my way out of the hospital I met Larry coming in. I told him you were asleep. (In fact, you would sleep through most of the night.) So he went in and kept your mother company until Kathleen would replace them early in the morning.

Friday
November 27

After 6:30 Mass, I quickly finished packing and was picked up at 7:30 for the ride to the airport. Just before I left, I phoned the hospital and asked the nurse to tell you I had phoned to say "good-bye," that I was leaving for the airport, and that I would phone from Missouri that evening.

The flight was a beautiful one in a small, six-seat craft. It was a sunny day and peaceful to be watching the fields and pastures as we passed over them, heading southwest.

It was during that flight that you died, Tom. Not long after the nurse passed my message on to you, your heart beat began to slow down and continued to do so until there was no beat left. Your sister Kathleen was with you. As she is a nurse, she knew you were in bad shape, so she left the room for a while and asked the good Lord to take you. A nurse asked her to return and shortly after that you died very peacefully. The doctor pronounced you dead at 10:20 a.m. It was your mother's birthday.

I didn't find out about it until I phoned after the ordination at about 9:30 that evening. I spoke to Florence, and she told me something I had already experienced. Sometimes people cannot die in the presence of someone to whom they are deeply attached. The attachment itself keeps them alive. So I guess you *couldn't* die until I left.

Normally grieving would have begun after the phone call, but most of my tears had been shed Tuesday morning. I was more numb than anything else—numbed because what I needed right then was space for a little quiet reflection, while my friend needed me to be a significant presence at his celebration which was going on all around me. To have to shift emotional gears back and forth between sorrow and joy, though it is an almost daily part of ministry, can prove too demanding at times. However, in your case, Tom, it was all right. For I was experiencing an expanding exaltation that filled me with awe at the beautiful way the Lord was continuing to handle everything: Your dying when you did was like his setting a divine seal on all that we shared.

When I was alone at last, it was still difficult to sort out the welter of emotions that was surging through me: sorrow at the loss of you, someone who meant so very much to me; joy because you were happy at last and beyond the reach of pain. I only knew that I was profoundly moved by all that had happened and that there were tears in my eyes as I fell asleep.

Sometimes in the weeks that followed, tears would well up unexpectedly. Once I remember it happening when for her first time I was giving a little girl the sacrament of reconciliation. She was smiling and so innocent, and there she was already beginning to wrestle with evil, having no idea how much pain would be mingled with the joy in her life. So my heart went out to her. Or perhaps it was *our* heart, Tom. . . .

Sunday
November 29

I took off from the Lebanon airport at about 1:00 p.m. During the flight home, while I was thinking about you, the Lord blessed me with the terrific realization that you had taken nearly two weeks of my life straight to heaven with you. Through you that much of my life is already living in glory. Surely if this is so, and I have no doubt that it is so, the rest of me will eventually follow. So I am going to heaven! It is not that in the past I had ever worried that I wouldn't go to heaven: I always hoped I would. But now I'm sure that I will. This doesn't leave me with the presumption that I am now free to do anything I please with the rest of my life. On the contrary, I treasure life now in a way I never could have imagined previously, and I want more than ever to live it well and to help others to do the same. And now I am more than simply grateful to the Lord. Having been so close to him for two weeks and having seen the way he manages things when given the chance, I am also beginning to love him much more deeply. "Can God be that good?" We both know that he *is*, Tom.

I arrived home late in the afternoon with just enough time to get to the rectory, change clothes, and go to the funeral home an hour before your family would arrive. I needed that hour so the two of us could spend a little time together in peace and quiet.

Then your family arrived. They seemed peaceful and happy to be together; a few tears, of course, but otherwise there were few obvious signs of sorrow. They are strong, good people, Tom, and I felt very close to them. I have since grown to love them.

The priests from St. Aidan came to the wake, and they led a beautiful prayer service. It was a quiet evening, since the wake had been unpublicized. Afterwards, we stopped at your house for coffee, and then it was time for sleep.

Monday
November 30

Your funeral Mass was at St. Aidan Church. I wanted to tell everyone about what we had shared, Tom, but that would have taken too long. The scripture readings I selected were Wisdom 4:7-14 (about the just man who dies young); 1 Corinthians 15:51-57 (about the glorification of the body and the victory of Christ over death); and John 20:19-31 (about the appearance of the risen Jesus to the disciples, especially Thomas, and his giving them his peace). I hoped my reflections on these readings and on your life managed to get across what I wanted to say. God is the one who touches hearts through the preaching of his word, and after all he had done for us, I couldn't doubt that he would inform each heart with what it most needed to hear.

There was another special manifestation, Tommy. The people! I don't know where they all came from, but there were hundreds and hundreds of them. The church was very nearly filled! As for the funeral procession to St. Mary's Cemetery, the line of cars stretched endlessly out of sight.

Endlessly out of sight in *both* directions stretched the heightened experience of our time together, which encompassed our two existences and fused them forever. It is said that, just before they die, people's lives flash before them in review. The extraordinary review we shared was a microcosm not only of our lives but of our place in the universe of God's love. Divine revelation broke forth like sunlight, striking the prism of the past; and what would otherwise have been a random sequence of half-forgotten memories flashed before us with the clarity and brilliance of the spectrum, compelling immediacy and perfect cohesion in an event that made our separate lives one and suspended us somewhere between time and eternity. It was as though we were meant to meet from the beginning, briefly on the threshold of death. Many pieces that never fit together before suddenly fell into place, because we understood that the word of God really *is* living and life-giving.

And when our paths parted again, yours took you on to eternity where, having suffered Christ's own sense of abandonment and having been touched by the power of his resurrection, you are now united with him in his compassionate love for the young, the lonely, and the depressed. Since you will always be with him, I cannot turn to you without also turning to him. Through his love, you will remain my life's special companion, one with him in desiring and striving for my well-being. I have never felt so loved or so trusted! And if I let you, you will lead me to those who need us most. My path brought me back to life here so I can share our gift with others and remind them that the Lord has planted the seeds of immortality in our own vulnerability.

It seems that the number of mourners has continued to increase, Tom. While this no longer matters to you, you cannot help but rejoice to know how many people have found new hope because of you. Wouldn't it be grand if, after having become acquainted with our story, they would be better able to realize how special and how cherished by God *they* are—that, in fact, they abide in the heart of God even more intimately than the unknowing infant lives in its mother's womb and is sustained by her being.

So much has resulted from a wise nurse's having done the right thing at the right time. Her faith told her that with God there is no such thing as "too late." So he made her his messenger. Indeed, she seemed to have had an inkling from the beginning that what had happened to you was to have a significance beyond itself. On the first day she phoned me, she said, "He's too special. . . . There *has* to be more for him. . . ." Recently, when I bumped into her in an elevator at the hospital, I thanked her for bringing us together and I told her that the whole experience had made a critical difference in my life. She gave me an enigmatic smile. "I know," she said. "It goes on like a song."

Lazarus

Having come forth once, my Lord, my Friend,
I await my second death
like a man who warms, smiles, whistles a little
as he wends his way,
after vagabond months and years of days,
to his loves, to his kin, to the lifebread of home.

Sister M. Pamela Smith, SSCM
from the book *Waymakers*